_____'s

SIGNS &
SKYMATES

RP Studio™
Hachette Book Group
1290 Avenue of the Americas, New York, NY 10104
www.runningpress.com
@Running_Press

Printed in China

First edition: December 2022

Published by RP Studio, an imprint of Perseus Books, LLC, a subsidiary of Hachette Book Group, Inc. The RP Studio name and logo are trademarks of the Hachette Book Group.

The publisher is not responsible for websites (or their content) that are not owned by the publisher.

Design by Susan Van Horn

ISBN: 978-0-7624-7805-7

1010

10 9 8 7 6 5 4 3 2 1

MY SIGNS & SKYMATES

A GUIDED JOURNAL FOR MAPPING YOUR ASTROLOGICAL COMPATIBILITY

DOSSÉ-VIA TRENOU

ILLUSTRATED BY NEKA KING

RP STUDIO

PHILADELPHIA

INTRODUCTION

From the astrological compatibility guide
Signs & Skymates, the companion to this journal...

Let me tell you a secret. The Universe wants you to feel love. It wants you to experience rich friendships. And it wants you to excel in whatever you decide to pursue. The Universe wants you to laugh your butt off at happy hour, and to feel vulnerable enough to let someone who loves you wipe away your tears at the crack of dawn. The Universe wants you to feel sexual bliss and intellectual stimulation. It wants you to travel, learn, teach, remember. It wants you to let yourself get angry, jealous, resentful, and passionate when those emotions come over you, and it also wants you to meditate, be still, and feel peace.

The Universe wants you to see yourself reflected within it. It's here to help you create a life you feel compatible with, while meeting and merging with those with whom you're most in tune. You've probably asked yourself the question, *"Well, who am I compatible with and how can I find them?"* You're in the right place. Several in-depth insights—and many more questions—await you as you embark on this journey. And by using the *Signs & Skymates* framework, you may very well have a path to finding your answers.

Guiding Questions for Using This Journal

Keep these questions in your mind as you work in this journal, and there will be space to reflect on them at the end.

* How can I apply my own values and perspective on astrological compatibility, which, like me, fluctuate and evolve with time, to my own romantic, professional, platonic, and widely changing array of relationships?

* Can I manifest my ideal partnerships (familial, platonic, professional, creative, and romantic) by getting to know myself more deeply first and foremost?

* Can I help others do the same, thus disrupting dangerous ideologies that mainstream astrology at times perpetuates?

Let's answer these questions together. View this journal as a conduit, a portal. But you are the guide, and your natal chart is the compass. Let's dive in.

SO YOU WANT
TO KNOW YOUR SKY, MATE?

Before we begin exploring your astrological compatibility with others, it's important to get to know your own cosmic self. Start by recording and reflecting on your Sun, Moon, and Rising signs. Then, use your information to look up a full natal chart, based on your time and place of birth.

BIRTH DATE
_____

PLACE OF BIRTH
_____

TIME OF BIRTH
_____

MY SUN SIGN
_____

MY MOON SIGN
_____

MY RISING SIGN (IF TIME IS KNOWN)
_____

What associations do you have with your Sun sign? Alternatively: What do you view as the main themes of your Sun sign?

_____

_____

_____

_____

_____

What associations do you have with your Moon sign? Alternatively: What do you view as the main themes of your Moon sign?

_____

_____

_____

_____

_____

What associations do you have with your Rising sign? Alternatively: What do you view as the main themes of your Rising sign?

_____

_____

_____

_____

_____

My Natal Chart

Use your date, place, and time of birth to construct a full natal chart for yourself—this is like a star map to your soul. Take that information and enter it into an online tool (you can find a birth chart calculator available at KnowTheZodiac.com), then record what you find in the blank natal chart on the next page.

♈ ARIES	♋ CANCER	♎ LIBRA	♑ CAPRICORN
♉ TAURUS	♌ LEO	♏ SCORPIO	♒ AQUARIUS
♊ GEMINI	♍ VIRGO	♐ SAGITTARIUS	♓ PISCES

Natal Chart Diagram

Leave houses blank if the time is unknown.

SUN	☉		in house
MOON	☽		in house
MERCURY	☿		in house
VENUS	♀		in house
MARS	♂		in house
JUPITER	♃		in house
SATURN	♄		in house
URANUS	♅		in house
NEPTUNE	♆		in house
PLUTO	♇		in house
NORTH NODE	☊		in house
SOUTH NODE	☋		in house
ASCENDANT	As	*The Rising sign always represents the first house of the self.*	in house *1*
MIDHEAVEN	MC	*The Midheaven always represents the tenth house of the career.*	in house *10*
CHIRON	⚷		in house
JUNO	⚵		in house

MY ASTROLOGICAL HOUSES: _____

MY PLANETARY ASPECTS: _____

MY STELLIUMS: _____

(A stellium is when three or more signs or houses repeat themselves in your chart. Please note that the lunar nodes, Midheaven, and asteroids aren't included when calculating stelliums. Some charts don't have any stelliums, and that's okay!)

What Is Astrological Compatibility and Why Does It Matter?

What exactly is compatibility? Think of it as a consistent sensation of feeling seen by someone or something, in a way that makes you feel at ease and allows you to reciprocate such energy. The word "consistent" is essential in this definition because it's the recurring aspect of feeling aligned with someone or something that helps maintain the feeling of compatibility.

Compatibility between humans is never set in stone. It's something that can be fine-tuned, but it takes patience, discipline, and an understanding and study of oneself and others to know which adjustments to make. And we may outgrow some friendships, family relationships, lovers, and partnerships, even if we once were tied at the hip.

Metaphysically, you could define compatibility as the synergy of one or more connections, with their energy vibrating off each other and creating another energy altogether. Even more than compatibility between human beings, compatibility has the range to explore the following:

❋ Compatibility with self, as a reminder that the most important relationship is the one you have with yourself, your values, your intention, and your love languages

❋ Compatibility with others, which can range from:
  - *Parents, siblings, family, co-parenting, blended families, etc.*
  - *Acquaintances, classmates/colleagues, friends, frenemies, enemies, etc.*
  - *Best friends, business partners, artistic collaborators, lovers, etc.*

* Compatibility with the day, week, or month itself

* Compatibility with a country or city (based on its independence/ conception day)

* Musical and artistic compatibility

* Career compatibility

* Compatibility with different life events, experiences, places, seasons, and cycles in your life

It's important to consider the whole chart when thinking about astrological compatibility. You will do yourself a disservice if you judge people based on their Sun signs only. The goal is to debunk the myths and highlight the infinite possibilities within a chart, and to celebrate the synergy and connections that two or more charts make with each other.

When you're looking at compatibility between two (or more) beings, you should absolutely try to include the other person in the process if possible.

As you begin this work, there are basic questions of compatibility that need to be addressed outside of astrological interpretations. Reflect on some of the relationships you're most interested in mapping.

My connection with

_____

What is the conception date of your connection (when did you two first meet or start talking)?

_____

_____

_____

_____

What are the strengths of your connection?

_____

_____

_____

_____

_____

_____

_____

_____

_____

_____

What brings you joy in your relationship?

What works about your connection?

My connection with

_____

What are the strengths of your connection?

_____
_____
_____
_____
_____
_____
_____
_____

What brings you joy in your relationship?

_____
_____
_____
_____
_____

What works about your connection?

Once you've gotten in the habit of observing the positives, communicate them to those around you whenever you notice what does work and flow. Once there is a baseline of highlighting strengths, it also becomes easier and less taboo to point out the areas that need work or readjustment.

Now that you've focused on the strengths, become aware of the areas of improvement that you notice within your connections with yourself and others. Start with yourself first, and then repeat the process with others.

My connection with

myself

What are the challenges of your connection?

_____

_____

_____

_____

_____

_____

_____

_____

What makes you feel most frequently frustrated or hurt in your relationship?

_____

_____

What would you to see improve and/or evolve within your connection?

My connection with

_____

What are the challenges of your connection?

_____

_____

_____

_____

_____

_____

_____

What makes you feel most frequently frustrated or hurt in your relationship?

_____

_____

_____

_____

What would you like to see improve and/or evolve within your connection?

My connection with

_____

What are the challenges of your connection?

_____

_____

_____

_____

_____

_____

_____

What makes you feel most frequently frustrated or hurt in your relationship?

_____

_____

_____

_____

What would you like to see improve and/or evolve within your connection?

THE FOUNDATIONS OF ASTROLOGY: ELEMENTS, SIGNS, HOUSES, PLANETS, PLACEMENTS & ASPECTS

In this section, you'll follow a compatibility formula that can be broken down into a 10-step process based on CONNECTION:

C : **Connect to your own chart first.**

O : **Open up to your primal triad (Sun, Moon, and Rising signs).**

N : **Now, look for recurring placements.**

N : **Next, study Mercury, Venus, and Mars placements.**

E : **Explore the relationships between the planets.**

C : **Connect the missing themes in your chart.**

T : **Time to pull up another's chart!**

I : **Interpret the information found in both charts (or more than two charts).**

O : **Organize the information based on what you've learned from each other.**

N : **Now comes the composite chart.**

Before you begin, please keep in mind that so many secrets and insights exist within our own chart, without even introducing the chart of another. But adding that additional chart can be powerful. Knowing the chart of another and comparing it with your own then becomes what we refer to as synastry. This journal includes elements of compatibility and synastry—the union of two charts. Composite compatibility is the union of two charts, while synastry is the alignment or misalignment of different charts' energies and the interpretation of the energy that those charts co-create.

C: Connect to Your Own Chart First

Refer to your chart on the "My Natal Chart" page.

WHAT PLANET IS YOUR CHART RULER(S)?_____

Your planetary ruler shows you what your priorities are. (Technically your chart ruler is based on your Rising sign, but since not everyone knows their Rising sign, you can also calculate your planetary ruler based on your Sun sign if need be.)

THE SIGNS AND THEIR PLANETARY RULERS

Aries ●—○ Mars

Taurus ●—○ Venus

Gemini ●—○ Mercury

Cancer ●—○ the Moon

Leo ●—○ the Sun

Virgo ●—○ Mercury

Libra ●—○ Venus

Scorpio ●—○ Mars & Pluto

Sagittarius ●—○ Jupiter

Capricorn ●—○ Saturn

Aquarius ●—○ Saturn & Uranus

Pisces ●—○ Jupiter & Neptune

MY (RISING/SUN) SIGN: _____

MY CHART RULER: _____

WHAT SIGN IS YOUR CHART RULER IN? _____
(This is whichever sign your chart ruler is placed in within your chart—this sign represents another sphere of influence in your chart.)

WHAT HOUSE PLACEMENT IS YOUR CHART RULER IN? _____
Note: House placements are accurate only if you know your specific birth time.

①: Open Up to Your Primal Triad

Make note of your Sun, Moon, and Rising (if known) signs, which you wrote down earlier. This is referred to as the "primal triad," and represents the core of your evolutionary personality, behavioral patterns, and temperament.

What do you already know about your primal triad? Where did your impressions of its meaning come from?

_____

_____

_____

_____

_____

_____

_____

_____

_____

_____

_____

_____

_____

_____

YOUR RISING SIGN: THE ASCENDANT

Your Rising sign symbolizes the first impression others have of you—sometimes without you being aware of it yourself—and it therefore has a considerable impact when it comes to who is attracted to us or repelled by us, and why. Having an awareness of your Rising sign helps you give yourself grace as you acknowledge the multiple layers of your personality. This is the mask you show the world, and only those who have the patience and courage to peel back the layers of that mask will get access to the totality of your essence (if you choose to grant them access).

WHAT IS YOUR RISING SIGN? _____

How do you think your Rising sign relates to how others perceive you?

_____

_____

_____

_____

_____

_____

_____

_____

_____

Even though a part of you may not necessarily identify with your Rising sign energy (if it's different from your Sun sign), it's helpful to develop an awareness that you present yourself that way, and that the energy of your Rising sign can even become a self-protective measure or disguise. Are there aspects of your Rising sign that you don't relate to? Reflect on them here.

On a more holistic level, our Rising sign is more than just the mask we present to the world. It can also be an indication of different themes we're meant to experience, learn, or unlearn during our time on Earth. What do you think you can learn from your Rising sign?

_____

_____

_____

_____

_____

_____

_____

_____

_____

_____

_____

_____

YOUR SUN SIGN: THE CORE, THE EGO STRUCTURE

Your Sun sign is the nucleus of your personality, and it's what most people think of when asked the question, "What's your sign?" It's therefore an opening to get an overall grasp on who we are as humans.

WHAT IS YOUR SUN SIGN? _____

Reflect on your Sun sign here. How does it resonate with you?

_____

_____

_____

_____

_____

_____

_____

_____

Just as the year is composed of different seasons, the twelve signs are representative of the four elements (Earth, Fire, Water, and Air).

WHAT ELEMENT IS YOUR SUN SIGN? _____

Reflect on the element of your Sun sign here. What aspects of its influence do you
see in yourself? Which don't you?

_____

_____

_____

_____

_____

_____

_____

WHAT IS THE HOUSE PLACEMENT OF YOUR SUN SIGN? _____

Study the themes of that specific house placement. In which ways have they played
out in your life? How has this house placement helped you on your evolutionary
journey, and in what ways may it sometimes appear to hinder your growth?

_____

_____

_____

_____

_____

_____

_____

YOUR MOON SIGN: THE LUMINARY OF YOUR EMOTIONS AND SUBCONSCIOUS

Our Moon signs influence our emotional responses to ourselves and others. The more attuned we are with our Moon sign, the more we hear our inner voice.

WHAT IS YOUR MOON SIGN? _____

Reflect on how you see your Moon sign in your emotional responses. Are there aspects of it that particularly resonate with you?

The Moon sign also represents our relationship to our mother, mother figures, or women in general. How do the themes of your Moon sign relate to how you feel about your mother, mother figures, or women in general?

_____

_____

_____

_____

_____

_____

_____

_____

_____

_____

_____

_____

_____

_____

_____

_____

The Moon's presence in each sign reflects a different emotional need that must be fulfilled for the Moon's power to be most potently expressed in our chart. What does your Moon sign tell you about what you need?

An understanding of Moon signs can also aid in figuring out how to show love and affection to people you love and want to receive affection from. Not everyone's love language is the same, and our Moon sign is a direct reflection of the diversity of ways of loving and being loved. How does your Moon sign influence your love language?

_____

_____

_____

_____

_____

_____

_____

_____

_____

_____

_____

_____

_____

_____

_____

_____

_____

WHAT IS THE HOUSE PLACEMENT OF YOUR MOON SIGN? _____

Study the themes of that specific house placement. In which ways have they played out in your life? How has this house placement helped you on your evolutionary journey, and in what ways, if any, may it sometimes appear to hinder your growth?

_____

_____

_____

_____

_____

_____

_____

_____

_____

_____

_____

_____

_____

_____

The Four Astrological Elements

The Fire signs are Aries, Leo, and Sagittarius. Skymates with these placements are inclined to show love through actions, boldness, adventure, and thrill. They encourage us to tap into our inner warriors.

What, if any, are the main Fire sign placements in your birth chart? In what ways has the element of Fire helped you on your evolutionary journey?

Which people in your life have Fire sign placements? How do they exhibit these qualities, or not? What can you learn from them?

The Earth signs are Taurus, Virgo, and Capricorn. Skymates with these placements demonstrate their love through practicality and precision. They remind us that staying rooted in who we are is a great way to ensure longevity in our objectives and that being too fixed in our belief systems can be detrimental and constraining.

What, if any, are the main Earth sign placements in your birth chart? In what ways has the element of Earth helped you on your evolutionary journey?

Which people in your life have Earth sign placements? How do they exhibit these qualities, or not? What can you learn from them?

The Air signs are Gemini, Libra, and Aquarius. Skymates with these placements are the communication experts, but part of their life lesson is to make sure their words have substance and depth, and that they're not simply talking to be heard. They encourage us to flow with change, rather than fight the currents of change, and remind us of the power of recognizing and exploring our malleable nature and flexible mindsets.

What, if any, are the main Air sign placements in your birth chart? In what ways has the element of Air helped you on your evolutionary journey?

Which people in your life have Air sign placements? How do they exhibit these qualities, or not? What can you learn from them?

_____

_____

_____

_____

_____

_____

_____

_____

_____

_____

_____

_____

_____

_____

_____

_____

_____

_____

The Water signs are Cancer, Scorpio, and Pisces. Skymates with these placements tend to love and live more emotively and intimately, sometimes to the point of being blindsided by their emotions and finding it hard to make practical decisions. They heal us and help us face our sensitivities with an increasing amount of clarity and self-trust.

What, if any, are the main Water sign placements in your birth chart? In what ways has the element of Water helped you on your evolutionary journey?

_____

_____

_____

_____

_____

_____

_____

_____

_____

_____

Which people in your life have Water sign placements? How do they exhibit these qualities, or not? What can you learn from them?

_____

_____

_____

_____

_____

_____

_____

_____

_____

_____

_____

_____

_____

_____

_____

_____

The Three Modalities

In addition to the four elements, the twelve zodiac signs are categorized into three different modes: Cardinal, Fixed, and Mutable. While elements show us the seasoning of these signs' personalities, the modes show us the direction in which their personality is aimed.

CARDINAL SIGNS: **Aries, Cancer, Libra, and Capricorn**

FIXED SIGNS: **Taurus, Leo, Scorpio, and Aquarius**

MUTABLE SIGNS: **Gemini, Virgo, Sagittarius, and Pisces**

What are the main modalities that are present in your chart?

CARDINAL PLACEMENTS:

_____

_____

FIXED PLACEMENTS:

_____

_____

MUTABLE PLACEMENTS:

_____

_____

The Cardinal signs are Aries, Cancer, Libra, and Capricorn. These signs are the initiators of the seasons—the ones who go after what they want even if they're unsure of how they'll get it. Masters of attraction and coordination, these team players know how to get things done, and their lives are a constant stream of adventures and possibilities.

Which people in your life have this energy? What can you learn from them?

The Fixed signs are Taurus, Leo, Scorpio, and Aquarius. These are the determined, stubborn signs—they exist in the middle of each season and use their discipline and foresight to see things through to completion after weeks or years of focus. These signs elicit very strong reactions from others—the response to a Fixed sign tends to be either love or hate, with hardly anything in between.

Which people in your life have this energy? What can you learn from them?

The Mutable signs are Gemini, Virgo, Sagittarius, and Pisces. The game-changers of the zodiac, Mutable signs conclude each season, reminding us of the transitional aspect of life and of ourselves. These adaptable skymates love taking in new information and have an intuitive understanding of death and rebirth.

Which people in your life have this energy? What can you learn from them?

_____

_____

_____

_____

_____

_____

_____

_____

_____

_____

_____

_____

_____

_____

_____

_____

_____

Ⓝ: Now Look at Your Recurring Placements

Look at which signs and house placements repeat themselves most. That's the core energy in your chart. Keep in mind that this is not always in the same sign as your Sun placement.

Having three or more placements in the same sign or house is called a stellium. We don't usually include the Midheaven, North Node, South Node, or asteroids when calculating stelliums.

> EXAMPLE: My Rising, Sun, Mercury, and Pluto placements are all in Scorpio. My Mercury, Venus, and Pluto placements are all in the first house of the self. Since the sign of Scorpio repeats itself three or more times in my chart, and the first house placement repeats itself three times as well, I have both a Scorpio stellium and a first house stellium.

What signs and house placements repeat in your chart?

_____

_____

_____

_____

_____

_____

What, if any, stelliums do you have?

N: Next, Look at Mercury, Venus, and Mars

Look at your Mercury, Venus, and Mars signs. These will show you key components of human relationships and relatability.

MY MERCURY SIGN:

MY VENUS SIGN:

MY MARS SIGN:

What do you already know about the significance of these placements in your chart? What impressions do you have of them?

YOUR MERCURY SIGN:
THE PLANET OF COMMUNICATION

In human relations, Mercury placement has quite an influence on how we get to know someone, what we think or infer about someone, and how we connect with them on a day-to-day level. It also helps us know which hobbies we're most drawn to, which educational paths we may want to take, and which careers will bring us intellectual satisfaction.

WHAT IS YOUR MERCURY SIGN? _____

Mercury placements inform which learning, writing, teaching, and working styles we're most compatible with. Looking at one's Mercury placement can help us better understand the environment we need to thrive mentally, feel safe, and open up to others.

Take a look at where Mercury is placed in your chart.

What does the sign and house tell you about the way you think and communicate with the world?

YOUR VENUS SIGN:
THE PLANET OF LOVE AND MAGNETISM

Even more than the Sun, Venus guides us toward knowing how to be in relationship with ourselves, others, animals, our consciousness, our material world, and the things we may not see. It is the planet of magnetism and social connection. It helps us attract money, beauty, luxury, wealth, abundance, and at times frivolity, overindulgence, jealousy, possessiveness, and passion.

WHAT IS YOUR VENUS SIGN? _____

Venus also searches for what feels good, looks good, and sounds good, at times being in denial of what is. But once the rose-colored glasses come off, she holds the mirror up and dares you to look within yourself, flaws and all.

Consider the areas of love, money, and indulgence ruled by Venus. Do you like what you see in these realms of your life? If not, why?

_____

_____

_____

_____

_____

_____

_____

_____

_____

Are you willing to be the change you wish to see in the realms of love, money, and indulgence? If not, why?

_____

_____

_____

_____

_____

_____

_____

_____

_____

_____

_____

_____

_____

_____

_____

The same question applies to all themes Venus rules: prosperity, money and our relationship to it, luxury, our own values. Reflect on those themes in your own life. Do you like what you see? Do you love who you are? What patterns of behavior do you notice about yourself, and are there any that you're seeking to change?

_____

_____

_____

_____

_____

_____

_____

_____

_____

_____

_____

Venus wants you to prioritize loving yourself in addition to loving others. She wants you to love yourself *through* loving others.

YOUR MARS SIGN:
THE PLANET OF ACTION, WAR, AND SEX

Mars is also associated with war, destruction and reconstruction, and the art and science of building things from the ground up. Mars is the cosmic force of activating energy that courses through us. It represents the actions we consistently take and the way we tend to take them. It also shows us the type of sex we're likely to want to have, or the types of partners we may be drawn to, as well as those who are drawn to us.

WHAT IS YOUR MARS SIGN AND HOUSE PLACEMENT? _____

Mars shows us what we'd be doing if we just let ourselves do it. It also shows us what we're afraid to do, even if we know that doing so would unlock another level of potential for us.

Reflect on those ideas here—how do you feel Mars's influence in these areas of your life?

_____

_____

_____

_____

_____

_____

_____

_____

_____

_____

Being aware of your Mars sign helps you better understand the tools it takes for you to successfully navigate and act in the world. It also provides insights on the types of people you tend to merge with or attract, and why.

Reflect on those ideas here—how do you feel Mars's influence in these areas of your life? Have you noticed that you tend to attract partners, friends, or colleagues who have key astrological placements in the same Mars sign as you? (Example: Someone with a Mars in Taurus may attract partners with major Taurus placements.)

E: Explore the Relationships between the Planets, Aspects, Signs, and Houses [P.A.S.H.]

Look at your chart and make a note of the relationships the planets were making with each other at the time of your birth. What geometric shapes, known as "planetary aspects," do you see?

(For information on aspects and what they look like, see the Aspects page at the back of the book.)

Make a note of your key astrological aspects below.

PLANETARY SEXTILES: _____

_____

_____

PLANETARY TRINES: _____

_____

_____

PLANETARY CONJUNCTIONS: _____

_____

_____

PLANETARY OPPOSITIONS: _____

_____

_____

PLANETARY SQUARES: _____

_____

_____

What were the planetary stories playing out in your life when you were born?

_____

_____

_____

_____

Were your key planets in harmony with each other (do you notice many sextiles and trines in your aspect chart)?

_____

_____

_____

_____

Were they more in union with each other (do you notice several conjunctions) or were they in discord (do you notice many oppositions or squares in your aspect chart)?

_____

_____

_____

For many charts it's often a blend of several energies, but some charts have a greater share of harmony and others a greater share of tension or challenging aspects. One type of chart is not better than the other, because even the most harmonious charts can experience trauma or hardship—and even the most challenging charts can experience moments of ease, love, and bliss.

If you've read the *Signs & Skymates* astrological compatibility guide as a complement to this journal, you can begin to think more broadly about aspects. List out the key aspects that stand out to you or that you'd like to make note of. Remember, you can take your time studying these. There's no need to rush through this process or overwhelm yourself. You can even study one aspect a day, or one aspect a month, if you'd like.

Below is an example of my personal aspects listed out. I enjoy both the periodic-table-like graphics, that are accessible via many online birth chart calculators, and I also enjoy listing them out for easy accessibility. Make note of your key aspects in whichever learning style speaks most to you—voice notes included!

EXAMPLE
✳ Moon sextile Mercury
✳ Moon sextile Pluto
✳ Moon sextile Mars
♂ Moon conjunct Jupiter
△ Mercury trine Mars
♂ Mercury conjunct Pluto
✳ Venus sextile Jupiter
△ Mars trine Ascendant
△ Mars trine Pluto
♂ Mars opposition Uranus
♂ Mars opposition Neptune
☐ Saturn square Ascendant

HOUSE PLACEMENTS:
WHERE WE DIRECT OUR SIGNS' ENERGY

In astrology, house placements tend to be some of the most significant parts of a chart. While the planets are the main characters, and the signs are the characters' archetypes, the house placements represent the thematic energy each planet and sign tends to be most drawn to. It helps us see what realm of life we may feel most at ease in, depending on our planetary sign and its house placement.

In compatibility, knowing your house placements can help you zero in on what you and your fellow skymates tend to invest most of your attention, energy, time, or resources in, as opposed to which sectors may not be of as much interest to you.

Refer back to your chart. What are your house placements?

THE FIRST HOUSE *(The House of the Self)* : _____

THE SECOND HOUSE *(The House of Money and Security)* : _____

THE THIRD HOUSE *(The House of Communication and Connection)* : _____

THE FOURTH HOUSE *(The House of the Home, the Past, and Our Roots)* : _____

THE FIFTH HOUSE *(The House of Pleasure, Fate, and Creativity)* : _____

THE SIXTH HOUSE *(The House of Service and Wellness)* : _____

THE SEVENTH HOUSE *(The House of Partnerships and Marriage)* : _____

THE EIGHTH HOUSE *(The House of Mergers, Depth, and Outside Resources)* : _____

THE NINTH HOUSE *(The House of Expansion, Travel, and Education)* : _____

THE TENTH HOUSE *(The House of Career and Reputation)* : _____

THE ELEVENTH HOUSE *(The House of Friendship and Social Networks)* : _____

THE TWELFTH HOUSE *(The House of Spirituality and Transcendence)* : _____

☾: Connect the Missing Themes in Your Chart

Which stories or themes seem to be missing from your chart?

_____

_____

_____

_____

_____

_____

_____

_____

_____

_____

_____

_____

_____

_____

_____

Which house placements and signs aren't as present in your chart?

_____

_____

_____

_____

_____

_____

_____

_____

_____

_____

_____

_____

These absences could indicate the types of people you would benefit from getting to know, in all sorts of ways—familiarly, romantically, spiritually. Conversely, you might butt heads with them because their energy isn't as present in your chart, so it can trigger discomfort.

Let's assess how much you're learning about your compatibility with yourself, based on everything you've read and learned so far. I'll present my own as an example.

Dossé-Via's Compatibility with Self:

✳ At my core (Sun sign), I have **Scorpio** energy, and since my Rising is **Scorpio**, I give off **Scorpio** vibes initially.

✳ The stelliums in my chart are my **Scorpio** energy (Sun, Rising, Mercury, Pluto), and my first house placements (Mercury, Venus, and Pluto).

✳ The house placements that aren't present in my chart are the **fourth, fifth, sixth, seventh, and eighth houses**, so I'd benefit from connecting with skymates who have those houses in their charts, or from infusing more energy from those house placements into my life.

✳ My planetary rulers are **Mars and Pluto**, so I should see which signs and houses they're placed in, because those placements have a strong influence on me and my evolution.

✳ My actions (Mars) come from a **Cancer**-like place, the way I love and attract things into my life (Venus) is **Sagittarius**-like, I attract luck (Jupiter) with **Libra** attributes, and I handle challenges (Saturn) from an **Aquarius**-like perspective.

✳ My planetary oppositions and squares in my chart may lead to feeling tension or conflict between my desire to be focused on **family-related** matters (Mars in Cancer) and my desire for **freedom and independence** (Uranus in Capricorn).

✳ The planetary trines in my chart bring harmony in my life when I seek out **honest, passionate communication** (Mercury in Scorpio) and **healing, nurturing environments** (Mars in Cancer).

✳ My elemental focus is **Water and Earth**, and I don't have as much Fire other than my Venus and North Node in Sagittarius and Midheaven in Leo placements.

✳ The planetary aspects that stand out to me most in my chart are: **Pluto square Chiron, Venus sextile Jupiter, Mars opposition Neptune, Mars opposition Uranus, North Node trine Midheaven, Mercury trine Mars, and Mars trine Pluto.**

Now it's your turn!

Your Compatibility with Self:

✳ At my core (Sun sign), I have _____ energy, and since my Rising is _____ , I give off _____ vibes initially. People may see me as_____.

✳ The stelliums in my chart (if any) are: _____

✳ The house placements that aren't present in my chart are _____ houses, so I'd benefit from connecting with skymates who have those houses in their charts, or from infusing more energy from those house placements into my life.

✳ My planetary ruler(s) are _____ , so I should see which signs and houses they're placed in, because those placements have a strong influence on me and my evolution.

✳ My actions (Mars) come from a _____ -like place, the way I love and attract things into my life (Venus) is _____ like, I attract luck (Jupiter) with _____ attributes, and I handle challenges (Saturn) from an _____ -like perspective.

✳ My planetary oppositions and squares (if any) in my chart may lead to me feeling tension or conflict between my desire to be focused on _____ matters and my desire for _____ .

✳ The planetary trines and sextiles (if any) in my chart bring harmony in my life when I seek out _____ and _____ .

✳ The main elements in my chart are: _____ .

✳ The planetary aspects that stand out to me most in my chart are: _____
_____ .

T : Time to Pull Up Another Person's Chart!

Now that you've studied and understood your own chart, inclinations in compatibility, main themes, and energies based off your chart placements, and what elements or themes seem to be missing, it's time to pull up other people's charts and repeat the same process! Ideally, they would do this process for themselves first, but you can also apply the steps above to interpret their chart on its own, without making a synastry or comparison to yours just yet. Get to know the individual chart's story first, without the need for it to be in relation to you. Let it live on its own, since we're all independent, unique beings who are in relationship with our own selves first and foremost.

Skymate #1:

_____

BIRTH DATE _____

PLACE OF BIRTH _____

TIME OF BIRTH _____

SUN SIGN _____

MOON SIGN _____

RISING SIGN _____

Conception date of your relationship (when did you two first meet or connect)? Why are you interested in mapping your compatibility with this person? What is your current impression of your relationship with them? What elements of this relationship are you most hoping to learn more about?

_____

_____

_____

_____

_____

_____

_____

_____

Natal Chart Diagram for:

SUN	◉		in house
MOON	☽		in house
MERCURY	☿		in house
VENUS	♀		in house
MARS	♂		in house
JUPITER	♃		in house
SATURN	♄		in house
URANUS	♅		in house
NEPTUNE	♆		in house
PLUTO	♇		in house
NORTH NODE	☊		in house
SOUTH NODE	☋		in house
ASCENDANT	As		in house *1*
MIDHEAVEN	MC		in house *10*
CHIRON	⚷		in house
JUNO	⚵		in house

THEIR ASTROLOGICAL HOUSES: _____

THEIR PLANETARY ASPECTS: _____

THEIR STELLIUMS: _____

Skymate #2:

_____

BIRTH DATE _____

PLACE OF BIRTH _____

TIME OF BIRTH _____

SUN SIGN _____

MOON SIGN _____

RISING SIGN _____

Conception date of your relationship (when did you two first meet or connect)? Why are you interested in mapping your compatibility with this person? What is your current impression of your relationship with them? What elements of this relationship are you most hoping to learn more about?

_____

_____

_____

_____

_____

_____

_____

_____

_____

Natal Chart Diagram for:

SUN	⊙		in house
MOON	☽		in house
MERCURY	☿		in house
VENUS	♀		in house
MARS	♂		in house
JUPITER	♃		in house
SATURN	♄		in house
URANUS	♅		in house
NEPTUNE	♆		in house
PLUTO	♇		in house
NORTH NODE	☊		in house
SOUTH NODE	☋		in house
ASCENDANT	As		in house *1*
MIDHEAVEN	MC		in house *10*
CHIRON	⚷		in house
JUNO	⚵		in house

THEIR ASTROLOGICAL HOUSES: _____

THEIR PLANETARY ASPECTS: _____

THEIR STELLIUMS: _____

Skymate #3:

_____

BIRTH DATE _____

PLACE OF BIRTH _____

TIME OF BIRTH _____

SUN SIGN _____

MOON SIGN _____

RISING SIGN _____

Conception date of your relationship (when did you two first meet or connect)? Why are you interested in mapping your compatibility with this person? What is your current impression of your relationship with them? What elements of this relationship are you most hoping to learn more about?

_____

_____

_____

_____

_____

_____

_____

_____

Natal Chart Diagram for:

SUN	☉		in house
MOON	☽		in house
MERCURY	☿		in house
VENUS	♀		in house
MARS	♂		in house
JUPITER	♃		in house
SATURN	♄		in house
URANUS	♅		in house
NEPTUNE	♆		in house
PLUTO	♇		in house
NORTH NODE	☊		in house
SOUTH NODE	☋		in house
ASCENDANT	As		in house *1*
MIDHEAVEN	MC		in house *10*
CHIRON	⚷		in house
JUNO	⚵		in house

THEIR ASTROLOGICAL HOUSES: _____

THEIR PLANETARY ASPECTS: _____

THEIR STELLIUMS: _____

Skymate #4:

_____

BIRTH DATE _____

PLACE OF BIRTH _____

TIME OF BIRTH _____

SUN SIGN _____

MOON SIGN _____

RISING SIGN _____

Conception date of your relationship (when did you two first meet or connect)?Why are you interested in mapping your compatibility with this person? What is your current impression of your relationship with them? What elements of this relationship are you most hoping to learn more about?

_____

_____

_____

_____

_____

_____

_____

_____

_____

_____

Natal Chart Diagram for:

SUN	☉		in house
MOON	☽		in house
MERCURY	☿		in house
VENUS	♀		in house
MARS	♂		in house
JUPITER	♃		in house
SATURN	♄		in house
URANUS	♅		in house
NEPTUNE	♆		in house
PLUTO	♇		in house
NORTH NODE	☊		in house
SOUTH NODE	☋		in house
ASCENDANT	As		in house *1*
MIDHEAVEN	MC		in house *10*
CHIRON	⚷		in house
JUNO	⚵		in house

THEIR ASTROLOGICAL HOUSES: _____

THEIR PLANETARY ASPECTS: _____

THEIR STELLIUMS: _____

⓵ : Interpret the Information in Two or More Charts Through Synastry

Look at your charts side by side. (You can always use the compatibility calculator at KnowTheZodiac.com or other online tools to pull up charts you may need for your analysis.) What strikes you first when you look at them? There are no right or wrong answers here. You may notice you both have the same Rising sign, or you both have Mars in Cancer, or that your Moon signs are in opposition to each other. Make note of what immediately comes up for you.

Keep in mind that if the time of birth is unknown you shouldn't be taking the Rising sign or house placements into account, and at times the Moon sign might not be fully accurate either.

⓪ : Organize the Information in Both Charts Based on What You've Learned from Each Other

Look at your Rising for the first impression you have of each other, and what your chart rulers are.

Next, look at the Sun to see the core of each other's external personalities; the Moon to see the emotional landscape with which you both live and the emotional and subconscious needs that must be met to feel safe in the relationship; and Mercury to see how you communicate with each other and the world.

Then look at Venus to see your dominant love languages and styles, to understand what you tend to attract as lovers, and the type of energy you are attracted to. Look at each other's Mars to understand the way you assert yourselves, or don't, in the world. Your Mars placements will indicate the types of actions each individual tends to take.

Do the same synastry analysis for house placements that you performed on your own chart. See things from the other person's chart and viewpoints. Ask them questions. Read their birth chart—swap birth charts and readings. Have fun exploring each other together!

Keep things neutral in your analysis, reminding yourself there are no good or bad placements. Just because a chart may have many oppositions with yours doesn't mean you'll never get along with that person.

SYNASTRY GUIDE FOR COMPATIBILITY WITH SKYMATES

Study these placements when trying to work out the recurring themes or areas of growth in your relationships:

MOTHER FIGURE = **the Moon / Neptune**

FATHER FIGURE = **the Sun / Saturn**

SIBLINGS = **Mercury + Saturn + signs and planets that activate your third house**

GRANDPARENTS = **Jupiter and Saturn placements and planetary aspects**

FRIENDS = **Rising, Mercury, Venus, Saturn, fifth-, and eleventh-house placements**

CO-WORKERS = **Rising, Mercury, Midheaven, Saturn, and tenth-house placements**

LOVERS = **Rising, Sun, Moon, Venus, Mars, Saturn, fourth-, fifth-, seventh-, and eighth-house placements, as well as your Juno and Chiron placements**

How to interpret three or more charts together: Use the same technique as with two synastry charts, and cross-compare to notice similarities and repeating themes or patterns.

Synastry with Skymate #1:

Synastry with Skymate #2:

Synastry with Skymate #3:

Synastry with Skymate #4:

Synastry notes:

Ⓝ: Now Comes the Composite Chart

While synastry charts are becoming more widely used in astrology, the composite chart is a lesser known, but equally valuable, aspect of astrological compatibility computation. A composite chart is calculated using the midpoints of two distinct charts to create a new chart, representative of the energy of the couple or partnership and what the relationship is here to teach us. We look at composite compatibility when assessing the long-term potential in a connection, such as best friends or marriage.

Unlike the synastry, which shows us the compatibility and chemistry between a couple, the composite chart is more about interpreting the reason why two beings came together, be it romantically, platonically, financially, or relationally. It highlights the struggles, strengths, areas of growth, overall dynamics, and purpose of a relationship, mapping its most essential themes and patterns.

How to Interpret a Composite Chart

1) Pay attention to the primary composite signs (Rising, Sun, Moon), houses, and aspects.

2) Pay attention to the chart ruler—where your relationship's energy is most frequently directed.

3) Focus on the placements of the Sun, Moon, Mercury, Venus, and Mars.

4) Pay attention to repeating elements, planetary aspects, and stelliums.

You can use the compatibility calculator at KnowTheZodiac.com to create composite charts.

Composite Chart with:

SUN	☉		in house
MOON	☽		in house
MERCURY	☿		in house
VENUS	♀		in house
MARS	♂		in house
JUPITER	♃		in house
SATURN	♄		in house
URANUS	♅		in house
NEPTUNE	♆		in house
PLUTO	♇		in house
NORTH NODE	☊		in house
SOUTH NODE	☋		in house
ASCENDANT	As		in house *1*
MIDHEAVEN	MC		in house *10*
CHIRON	⚷		in house
JUNO	⚵		in house

OUR ASTROLOGICAL HOUSES: _____

OUR PLANETARY ASPECTS: _____

OUR STELLIUMS: _____

Notes

Composite Chart with:

SUN	☉		in house
MOON	☽		in house
MERCURY	☿		in house
VENUS	♀		in house
MARS	♂		in house
JUPITER	♃		in house
SATURN	♄		in house
URANUS	♅		in house
NEPTUNE	♆		in house
PLUTO	♇		in house
NORTH NODE	☊		in house
SOUTH NODE	☋		in house
ASCENDANT	As		in house *1*
MIDHEAVEN	MC		in house *10*
CHIRON	⚷		in house
JUNO	⚵		in house

OUR ASTROLOGICAL HOUSES: _____

OUR PLANETARY ASPECTS: _____

OUR STELLIUMS: _____

Notes

Composite Chart with:

SUN	☉		in house
MOON	☽		in house
MERCURY	☿		in house
VENUS	♀		in house
MARS	♂		in house
JUPITER	♃		in house
SATURN	♄		in house
URANUS	♅		in house
NEPTUNE	♆		in house
PLUTO	♇		in house
NORTH NODE	☊		in house
SOUTH NODE	☋		in house
ASCENDANT	As		in house *1*
MIDHEAVEN	MC		in house *10*
CHIRON	⚷		in house
JUNO	⚵		in house

OUR ASTROLOGICAL HOUSES: _____

OUR PLANETARY ASPECTS: _____

OUR STELLIUMS: _____

Notes

Composite Chart with:

SUN	☉		in house
MOON	☽		in house
MERCURY	☿		in house
VENUS	♀		in house
MARS	♂		in house
JUPITER	♃		in house
SATURN	♄		in house
URANUS	♅		in house
NEPTUNE	♆		in house
PLUTO	♇		in house
NORTH NODE	☊		in house
SOUTH NODE	☋		in house
ASCENDANT	As		in house *1*
MIDHEAVEN	MC		in house *10*
CHIRON	⚷		in house
JUNO	⚵		in house

OUR ASTROLOGICAL HOUSES: _____

OUR PLANETARY ASPECTS: _____

OUR STELLIUMS: _____

Notes

Composite Chart Analysis
The Composite Placements

COMPOSITE ASCENDANT/ RISING PLACEMENTS
THE FIRST IMPRESSION OTHERS HAVE OF YOUR CONNECTION

The composite Ascendant symbolizes how people first view you as a pair, as well as the type of place or circumstance in which you met or your relationship developed. It also highlights the day-to-day attitudes and habits you have together and how you relate to each other.

COMPOSITE SUN PLACEMENTS
THE CORE OF YOUR RELATIONSHIP

The composite Sun is the midpoint of two individual Sun signs and usually different from either of them. This makes it very compelling to study because a new core personality is created, forming the nucleus of the connection.

COMPOSITE MOON PLACEMENTS
YOUR COMBINED EMOTIONAL NEEDS

The composite Moon refers to what your relationship's emotional needs are—not your individual needs, but what your union needs to be emotionally fulfilled as a couple. It also highlights the approach you may take for tackling emotional responsibilities or expressing yourselves emotively.

COMPOSITE MERCURY PLACEMENT
YOUR COMBINED COMMUNICATION NEEDS

The Composite Mercury placement shows skymates how they relate to each other intellectually. It highlights the pairing's communication style as well as the main themes they might primarily discuss. Skymates who study this composite placement can gain awareness about the best way to exchange ideas, from making dinner suggestions to brainstorming business endeavors together.

COMPOSITE VENUS PLACEMENTS
YOUR COMBINED RELATIONAL NEEDS

The composite Venus informs what your pairing needs to feel socially fulfilled and mutually seen, celebrated, and loved. Venus is often looked to as central in romantic interpretations, but it's an essential part of platonic relationships as well.

COMPOSITE MARS PLACEMENTS
YOUR COMBINED ACTIONS

The composite Mars highlights your relationship's actions and life force and shows what energizes the partnership. If it's a romantic connection, the composite Mars concerns your sex life. It also informs how a pair expresses anger or frustration in their relationship.

COMPOSITE JUPITER PLACEMENTS
HOW YOUR PAIRING IS MEANT TO ATTRACT ABUNDANCE AND LUCK

In the composite chart, Jupiter, the Planet of Luck, shows us what themes or situations bring the relationship opportunities for expansion. It also serves as a warning of when a pair of skymates may be pushing their luck by being overly indulgent.

COMPOSITE SATURN PLACEMENTS
HOW YOUR RELATIONSHIP GROWS, OR STALLS, DUE TO CHALLENGE

The composite Saturn acknowledges the most challenging parts of your relationship and what tools you'll need to overcome them. It can also show us what may push a relationship to its breaking point if left unacknowledged.

THE COMPOSITE CHIRON
THE HEALING JOURNEY OF YOUR RELATIONSHIP

Look to your composite Chiron for where your relationship's deepest wounds may be, as well as the themes or traumas you'll have to unpack to ensure its longevity and healing.

THE COMPOSITE NORTH NODE
THE DESTINY OF YOUR RELATIONSHIP

Your composite North Node is an indication of what your long-term purpose may be as a pair. It helps you map out your legacy and influence in the world when you combine your energies.

THE COMPOSITE SOUTH NODE
THE KARMIC PAST OF YOUR RELATIONSHIP

The South Node is the opposite sign of your North Node placement, and this composite placement sheds light on what the past-life energy of your connection may stem from. It also reveals unfinished business that may exist within the relationship, which could manifest as karmic wounds or karmic opportunities to heal those wounds.

The Composite Houses

The houses in a composite chart highlight where the energy from your composite signs are most directed, and what you can offer each other as a result of that realm of focus.

THE COMPOSITE FIRST HOUSE
THE HOUSE OF SELF

If a couple has any of the personal planets (Sun, Moon, Mercury, Venus, Mars) in the first house, or if their composite chart's planetary ruler is placed there, their relationship emanates "big main character energy." They're curious about getting to know each other and enjoy being seen together. They must be sure they're not so focused on themselves that they forget to pay attention to their other interactions.

THE COMPOSITE SECOND HOUSE
THE HOUSE OF SECURITY

The composite second house helps partners with this placement learn the true value of security. This can be a financially savvy placement but can also lead to partners needing to face the truth about their financial reality and knowing their worth beyond it. Emotional security is also a key point of this house placement—these skymates may feel an urge to be sure of each other's commitment, or to know each other's true feelings. The key is for them to figure out their own feelings before requesting transparency from another.

THE COMPOSITE THIRD HOUSE
THE HOUSE OF COMMUNICATION

Having prominent third house placements in a composite chart indicates that communication is a central theme—but it doesn't necessarily indicate that the skymates will always have the smoothest interactions. They'll have to look at how the specific signs and houses are interacting in their composite chart to get a better sense of that. No matter what, connecting through creation, be it oral, artistic, written, or musical, is an inherent need in this pairing.

THE COMPOSITE FOURTH HOUSE
THE HOUSE OF THE HOME

Wherever the composite fourth house is placed indicates the realms of the connection that will pay most attention to family- and values-related ideals. Since the fourth is one of the foundational houses, addressing any pent-up issues in the couple's individual and joint past, real-estate investments, values, and traumas will be key to maintaining longevity and a healthy, prosperous connection.

THE COMPOSITE FIFTH HOUSE
THE HOUSE OF FATE, PLEASURE, AND ADVENTURE

The Composite fifth house is where we look to bring more pleasure, creativity, youthfulness, and brightness into the partnership. Depending on where it's placed in their chart, this house can also highlight when the couple needs to tap into these themes to keep the vibrancy and life force alive in the partnership. Fifth-house energy plays a strong role in romantic compatibility, but often indicates more short-term passions and interests.

THE COMPOSITE SIXTH HOUSE
THE HOUSE OF WELLNESS AND HEALING

The composite sixth house asks the couple to check in on their mental, physical, and spiritual health and well-being, but it cautions them against doing so in an obsessive, mutually overwhelming way. Skymates with prominent sixth-house energy in their composite chart will want the best for each other, but at times they'll focus too much on what seems to not be working. Rather than try to "fix" each other, they must accept each other's flaws.

THE COMPOSITE SEVENTH HOUSE
THE HOUSE OF MARRIAGE AND PARTNERSHIP

The composite seventh house indicates the way we relate to ourselves and to other beings outside of our partnership. One of the biggest evolutionary lessons of composite seventh-house placements is accepting each other as they are. These partners thrive when they avoid getting caught up in ideals of who they wish the other could be.

THE COMPOSITE EIGHTH HOUSE
THE HOUSE OF MERGING AND INTIMACY

Couples with a composite eighth-house placement in their chart will often want to merge with each other—mind, body, and soul. Their energy oozes with intensity, and they'll have to guard against being overly secretive with or possessive of each other. One of their evolutionary lessons will be to respect each other's boundaries and each be their own person.

THE COMPOSITE NINTH HOUSE
THE HOUSE OF EXPANSION
AND LONG JOURNEYS

Skymates with prominent ninth-house placements in their composite chart were brought together to explore travel, entrepreneurship, philosophy, spirituality, and knowledge. They share an inherent insatiability, and their relationship can be as adventurous as they allow themselves to be. These skymates' relationships will deepen as they step out of their comfort zone.

THE COMPOSITE TENTH HOUSE
THE HOUSE OF CAREER
AND REPUTATION

Skymates with prominent tenth-house placements in their composite chart probably pay a significant amount of attention to their joint career goals, as well as their reputation and social standing. While these skymates have the potential to make great progress on joint endeavors, they also run the risk of becoming workaholics, or placing too much pressure on each other to succeed in that realm.

THE COMPOSITE ELEVENTH HOUSE
THE HOUSE OF FRIENDSHIP
AND SOCIAL NETWORKS

The composite eleventh house has to do with our social and in-person networks, the communities we choose to identify with, and the causes we choose to champion—as well as the ones that we don't. This placement may indicate that friendship is a foundation for the relationship and should be prioritized before any other relationship grows. Skymates with eleventh-house composite energy often enjoy committing to humanitarian causes, and together they can lead the way.

THE COMPOSITE TWELFTH HOUSE
THE HOUSE OF SPIRITUALITY
AND HEALING

Composite chart placements in the twelfth house indicate elusiveness, secrecy, and depth in the connection. There may be aspects of this pair that seem mysterious to others—even those who have known them for a while. This placement can be emotionally intense and there's a risk of falling into codependent patterns or using drugs, alcohol, food, sleep, or sex to escape reality together, but they also often share amazing artistic and healing abilities.

WHAT COMPOSITE STELLIUMS MEAN

Pay attention to where signs or house placements repeat themselves three or more times in a composite chart. Just as stelliums in one's personal chart indicate areas of emphasis, stelliums in a composite chart reveal the most pressing themes and experiences in the couple's relationship. Make note of any stelliums in your composite chart, as you'd benefit from studying those placements to figure out your long-term compatibility and potential as partners.

———✳———

It's your turn now. Using the information you've learned from synastry and composite charts, assess the relational themes that are being revealed to you through your composite and synastry charts. Remember that it is the skymates themselves who bring life to their charts, and not the other way around. Be reflective about your connection(s) with other skymates and be present with them too.

Compatibility with Another:

1) Trust your instincts and your own primal astrological wisdom as you look at your chart alongside another's. What do you first notice? What story can you already see through the elements and configurations of both of your placements? Trust yourself and your subconscious—it knows more than your rational mind.

2) If you're reading your charts with your partner(s), have them make note of their initial impressions of your chart(s). They can do this even if they don't know much about astrology. Perhaps they'll notice that you both have the same sign that pops up a lot, or the same house placements. Let them pay attention to the signs too.

3) What are your primal triads (Sun, Moon, Rising)?

_____

4) What are your planetary rulers? (Look at your Rising signs and see which planet(s) rule those signs. Then, see which sign that planet is in for each of your charts (in synastry) or your composite chart. Example: If you're an Aries Rising, you'll look at where Mars, Aries's planetary ruler, is placed in your chart. If Mars is placed in Leo, then you'd be deeply influenced by Leo energy.

_____

5) Which sign or house placements, if any, do you and your partner(s) share?

_____

_____

_____

_____

_____

_____

_____

_____

_____

_____

_____

_____

6) Which sign or house placements form an opposition, trine, sextile, conjunction, or square with each other? In what ways have the planetary aspects in your partnership influenced key patterns in your relationship?

_____

_____

_____

_____

_____

_____

7) Which houses/sectors of your chart are activated by each other (this can only be calculated if both times of births are known)?

_____

_____

_____

_____

_____

_____

_____

_____

_____

_____

Compatibility with Another:

1) Trust your instincts and your own primal astrological wisdom as you look at your chart alongside another's. What do you first notice? What story can you already see through the elements and configurations of both of your placements? Trust yourself and your subconscious—it knows more than your rational mind.

2) If you're reading your charts with your partner(s), have them make note of their initial impressions of your chart(s). They can do this even if they don't know much about astrology. Perhaps they'll notice that you both have the same sign that pops up a lot, or the same house placements. Let them pay attention to the signs too.

3) What are your primal triads (Sun, Moon, Rising)?

_____

4) What are your planetary rulers? (Look at your Rising signs and see which plan-
   et(s) rule those signs. Then, see which sign that planet is in for each of your
   charts (in synastry) or your composite chart. Example: If you're an Aries Rising,
   you'll look at where Mars, Aries's planetary ruler, is placed in your chart. If Mars
   is placed in Leo, then you'd be deeply influenced by Leo energy.

_____

5) Which sign or house placements, if any, do you and your partner(s) share?

_____

_____

_____

_____

_____

_____

_____

_____

_____

_____

_____

_____

6) Which sign or house placements form an opposition, trine, sextile, conjunction, or square with each other? In what ways have the planetary aspects in your partnership influenced key patterns in your relationship?

_____

_____

_____

_____

_____

_____

7) Which houses/sectors of your chart are activated by each other (this can only be calculated if both times of births are known)?

_____

_____

_____

_____

_____

_____

_____

_____

_____

_____

_____

Compatibility with Another:

1) Trust your instincts and your own primal astrological wisdom as you look at your chart alongside another's. What do you first notice? What story can you already see through the elements and configurations of both of your placements? Trust yourself and your subconscious—it knows more than your rational mind.

2) If you're reading your charts with your partner(s), have them make note of their initial impressions of your chart(s). They can do this even if they don't know much about astrology. Perhaps they'll notice that you both have the same sign that pops up a lot, or the same house placements. Let them pay attention to the signs too.

3) What are your primal triads (Sun, Moon, Rising)?

_____

4) What are your planetary rulers? (Look at your Rising signs and see which plan-
et(s) rule those signs. Then, see which sign that planet is in for each of your
charts (in synastry) or your composite chart. Example: If you're an Aries Rising,
you'll look at where Mars, Aries's planetary ruler, is placed in your chart. If Mars
is placed in Leo, then you'd be deeply influenced by Leo energy.

_____

5) Which sign or house placements, if any, do you and your partner(s) share?

_____

_____

_____

_____

_____

_____

_____

_____

_____

_____

_____

_____

6) Which sign or house placements form an opposition, trine, sextile, conjunction, or square with each other? In what ways have the planetary aspects in your partnership influenced key patterns in your relationship?

_____

_____

_____

_____

_____

_____

7) Which houses/sectors of your chart are activated by each other (this can only be calculated if both times of births are known)?

_____

_____

_____

_____

_____

_____

_____

_____

_____

_____

Compatibility with Another:

1) Trust your instincts and your own primal astrological wisdom as you look at your chart alongside another's. What do you first notice? What story can you already see through the elements and configurations of both of your placements? Trust yourself and your subconscious—it knows more than your rational mind.

2) If you're reading your charts with your partner(s), have them make note of their initial impressions of your chart(s). They can do this even if they don't know much about astrology. Perhaps they'll notice that you both have the same sign that pops up a lot, or the same house placements. Let them pay attention to the signs too.

3) What are your primal triads (Sun, Moon, Rising)?

_____

4) What are your planetary rulers? (Look at your Rising signs and see which planet(s) rule those signs. Then, see which sign that planet is in for each of your charts (in synastry) or your composite chart. Example: If you're an Aries Rising, you'll look at where Mars, Aries's planetary ruler, is placed in your chart. If Mars is placed in Leo, then you'd be deeply influenced by Leo energy.

_____

5) Which sign or house placements, if any, do you and your partner(s) share?

_____

_____

_____

_____

_____

_____

_____

_____

_____

_____

_____

6) Which sign or house placements form an opposition, trine, sextile, conjunction, or square with each other? In what ways have the planetary aspects in your partnership influenced key patterns in your relationship?

_____

_____

_____

_____

_____

_____

7) Which houses/sectors of your chart are activated by each other (this can only be calculated if both times of births are known)?

_____

_____

_____

_____

_____

_____

_____

_____

_____

_____

Are you ready to do the work?

Now that you know better, are you ready to move better?

Skymates, it's time to check in with yourself. Use these pages to reflect on your past through the lens of the insights you've gained through mapping compatibility found in this journal and in *Signs & Skymates*.

Look at your past journals. Write a timeline of what happened in the relationships that have left the biggest impact on your soul, your mind, and your consciousness. Create a story of what happened—one that makes sense to you, even if it has plenty of plot holes or contradictions. Notice the patterns. Focus on what you accepted. Try not to shame yourself for what you accepted, but instead, take responsibility for the choices you made when you were in that relationship. Be honest if you may need help from a professional therapist in order to healthfully process your trauma or pain. Then decide how you want to move forward. Decide how you want to experience love from this point on. Decide the type of lover(s) you'd like to merge with from this point on. If you're still in one of those relationships, or many, and you're ready to do the work together to evolve, be honest and stay focused on that. Don't let the past versions of who you and your partner(s) were cloud your judgment or your ability to transform, grow, and let go. While for some it takes time, this process of doing the work can also happen overnight. Some people suddenly have an epiphany, perhaps through reading sentences in a book, and voilà! It may also take weeks, months, or years. It doesn't matter how long it takes. What matters is that you commit to the mission of choosing yourself, acknowledging your needs, taking accountability for your decisions, and daring to begin again, using your natal chart and divine intuition as guiding tools that remind you of your ever-expansive essence.

Astrological Plot Twists

Think of the plot twists that have occurred in your romantic, familial, friend-ship, or professional life over the course of your journey. Record the dates and include the astrological info of whomever the plot twist occurred with, as well as any cosmic insights about the date or season. What insights can be gained when you consider the experience through the lens of astrological compatibility, using what you've learned?

DATE: _____

WHAT HAPPENED: _____

_____

_____

_____

_____

_____

_____

_____

_____

_____

_____

_____

_____

_____

_____

WHAT SIGN'S ASTROLOGICAL SEASON WAS IT? _____

DOES THAT SIGN ACTIVATE ANY HOUSES IN YOUR CHART? _____

WITH WHOM DID THE PLOT TWIST OCCUR? _____

THEIR ASTROLOGICAL INFO: _____

REFLECTIONS: _____

DATE: _____

WHAT HAPPENED: _____

_____

_____

_____

_____

_____

_____

_____

_____

_____

_____

_____

_____

_____

WHAT SIGN'S ASTROLOGICAL SEASON WAS IT? _____

DOES THAT SIGN ACTIVATE ANY HOUSES IN YOUR CHART? _____

WITH WHOM DID THE PLOT TWIST OCCUR? _____

THEIR ASTROLOGICAL INFO: _____

REFLECTIONS: _____

DATE: _____

WHAT HAPPENED: _____

_____

_____

_____

_____

_____

_____

_____

_____

_____

_____

_____

_____

_____

_____

WHAT SIGN'S ASTROLOGICAL SEASON WAS IT? _____

DOES THAT SIGN ACTIVATE ANY HOUSES IN YOUR CHART? _____

WITH WHOM DID THE PLOT TWIST OCCUR? _____

THEIR ASTROLOGICAL INFO: _____

REFLECTIONS: _____

_____

_____

_____

_____

_____

_____

_____

_____

_____

_____

_____

_____

_____

_____

_____

_____

_____

_____

_____

_____

DATE: _____

WHAT HAPPENED: _____

_____

_____

_____

_____

_____

_____

_____

_____

_____

_____

_____

_____

_____

WHAT SIGN'S ASTROLOGICAL SEASON WAS IT? _____

DOES THAT SIGN ACTIVATE ANY HOUSES IN YOUR CHART? _____

WITH WHOM DID THE PLOT TWIST OCCUR? _____

THEIR ASTROLOGICAL INFO: _____

REFLECTIONS: _____

Using what you've learned, let's reflect on the guiding questions from the beginning of this journal.

How can I apply my own values and perspective on astrological compatibility—which, like me, fluctuate and evolve with time—to my own romantic, professional, platonic, and widely changing array of relationships?

Can I manifest my ideal partnerships (familial, platonic, professional, creative, and romantic) by getting to know myself more deeply first and foremost?

Can I help others manifest their ideal partnerships, thus disrupting dangerous ideologies that mainstream astrology at times perpetuates?

Here are some affirmations to remind yourself of your birth chart's ability to activate your most divine potential and most aligned relationships:

UNIVERSAL AFFIRMATIONS

I have faith in life.

I trust myself, the Universe, and my evolution.

I am learning to be attracted to what's healing and empowering for me.

I am committed to unlearning harmful ideologies and rooting myself in my core values.

I welcome my own shadows, and I have awareness for the shadows of humanity.

I am open and ready to do the work, and whenever I'm not ready, I give myself grace.

Write your own universal affirmations to help you affirm your magic.

My Compatibility Insights

If you are reading my compatibility guide *Signs & Skymates*, use these pages to jot down the compatibility insights and excerpts that speak to you the most. Otherwise, use this space as additional room for exploring the journaling prompts from the preceding pages.

REFERENCES
The Signs & Their Planetary Rulers

Please note that the beginning and ending dates of each astrological season are approximate, because the Sun enters each sign at a different time, and sometimes a slightly different date, each year.

Aries	*March 21– April 19*	ruled by Mars, the Planet of Action
Taurus	*April 20– May 20*	ruled by Venus, the Planet of Love and Magentism
Gemini	*May 21– June 20*	ruled by Mercury, the Planet of Communication
Cancer	*June 21– July 22*	ruled by the Moon, the Luminary of Sensitivity
Leo	*July 23– August 22*	ruled by the Sun, the Luminary of Essence
Virgo	*August 23– September 22*	ruled by Mercury, the Planet of Communication
Libra	*September 23– October 22*	ruled by Venus, the Planet of Love and Magnetism
Scorpio	*October 23– November 22*	ruled by Mars, the Planet of Action, and Pluto, the Planet of Transformation
Sagittarius	*November 22– December 20*	ruled by Jupiter, the Planet of Expansion
Capricorn	*December 21– January 19*	ruled by Saturn, the Planet of Challenge
Aquarius	*January 20– February 18*	ruled by Saturn, the Planet of Responsibility, and Uranus, the Planet of Revolution
Pisces	*February 19– March 20*	ruled by Jupiter, the Planet of Expansion, and Neptune, the Planet of Fantasy

Planets in Detriment

Planets feel awkward, or in astrology-speak they are "in detriment," when placed in the signs that are the opposite of their planetary ruler:

Sun ✳	Aquarius
Moon ✳	Capricorn
Mercury ✳	Sagittarius and Pisces
Venus ✳	Aries and Scorpio
Mars ✳	Taurus and Libra
Jupiter ✳	Gemini and Virgo
Saturn ✳	Cancer and Leo

Planets in Exaltation

Sometimes the opposite is true, and planets are placed in a sign that inclines them to feel high off of life and there is a greater feeling of ease and familiarity when the planet is in that sign—even though that is not that planet's actual ruler. Such placements are viewed as planets being "exalted" in that sign:

Sun ✳	Aries
Moon ✳	Taurus
Mercury ✳	Virgo
Venus ✳	Pisces
Mars ✳	Capricorn
Jupiter ✳	Cancer
Saturn ✳	Libra

Planets in Their Fall

There are times when a planet isn't able to function to its strongest capacity because of the sign in which it's placed. This is referred to as a planet being in its "fall." If you place the signs in a circle, in order, you'll find the signs that are directly opposite one another, and a planet's "fall" is directly opposite its exalted placements:

Sun ✳	Libra
Moon ✳	Scorpio
Mercury ✳	Pisces
Venus ✳	Virgo
Mars ✳	Cancer
Jupiter ✳	Capricorn
Saturn ✳	Aries

Aspects

Below are the five most common types of major planetary aspects found in birth charts (which we also analyze in synastry and composite compatibility charts):

Trines

This aspect is smooth-sailing harmony, with planets being at a 120-degree angle to each other. An abundance of planetary trines in one's birth chart can lead to people taking certain blessings in their lives for granted or feeling like there's no need to put in concerted effort in a specific direction. But when one is aware of the planetary trines in their personal and/or synastry and composite charts, they can rely on them when they need a boost in morale. Trines serve as sweet spots in one's chart, reminding us that life can be easeful sometimes, and we can all just chill and appreciate the good vibes.

Sextiles

A 60-degree angle between planets represents ease and bliss, but at times too many of these aspects can lead to the skymate feeling that everything comes easily to them, or even that life's too smooth sailing, which can cause them to seek out drama to spice up their life, either consciously or unconsciously.

Conjunctions

Made of zero-degree angles, this aspect occurs most often when the planets are in the same signs. While this tends to be associated with neutral energy, the real energetic influence of the conjunction depends on which planets are in conjunction with each other. The Moon and Venus conjoining in the same sign can increase someone's sex appeal and emotional expressions, while a Moon and Saturn conjunction could increase their self-criticism or make them less emotionally expressive, due to Saturn being a more challenging planet than Venus.